EDGE
BOOKS™

ALL
ABOUT
DOGS

SHIH TZUS

By Brekka Hervey Larrew

Consultant: Jo Ann White
Author, *The Official Book of the Shih Tzu*

Capstone
press®

Mankato, Minnesota

Edge Books are published by Capstone Press,
151 Good Counsel Drive, P.O. Box 669, Mankato, Minnesota 56002.
www.capstonepress.com

Library of Congress Cataloging-in-Publication Data
Larrew, Brekka Hervey.
    Shih tzus / by Brekka Hervey Larrew.
    p. cm. — (Edge books. All about dogs.)
    Includes bibliographical references and index.
    ISBN-13: 978-1-4296-1950-9 (hardcover)
    ISBN-10: 1-4296-1950-3 (hardcover)
    1. Shih tzu — Juvenile literature. I. Title. II. Series.
SF429.S64L37 2009
636.76 — dc22   2008001203

Summary: Describes the history, physical features, temperament, and care of
    the shih tzu breed.

Editorial Credits
Erika L. Shores, editor; Veronica Bianchini, designer; Marcie Spence,
    photo researcher

Photo Credits
Alamy/Pegaz, 5
BigStockPhoto.com/Kara Edwards, 29
Capstone Press/Karon Dubke, cover, 1, 8, 10, 13, 14, 16, 17, 18, 20, 23, 24, 26
Corbis/Robert Dowling, 21
Getty Images Inc./Carl Mydans/Time Life Pictures, 12; Ernst Haas, 9
iStockphoto/niknikon, 7
Landov LLC/Alessia Pierdomenico/Reuters, 25
Shutterstock/Margot Petrowski, 15; Mikhail Levit, 11

**Consultant Jo Ann White encourages anyone interested in learning more about
    the shih tzu breed to visit the American Shih Tzu Club web site at
    www.shihtzu.org.**

**Capstone Press thanks Martha Diedrich, dog trainer, for her assistance
    with this book.**

1 2 3 4 5 6 13 12 11 10 09 08

Table of Contents

CHAPTER 1

A PET FIT FOR A KING

For hundreds of years, Chinese **emperors** valued fluffy, friendly lapdogs. To satisfy their desire for canine companions, they bred the shih tzu. They especially loved how the shih tzu's long hair made it look like a lion. In fact, shih tzu means lion in Chinese.

The shih tzu is among the most ancient of all dog breeds. Bred to be a pet, it loves people. This small dog also has a proud, stubborn streak. A shih tzu's personality makes it seem almost human. These qualities help make these little dogs such popular pets.

Does a shih tzu sound like your kind of pet? Adopting a dog can be an exciting experience for a family. Shih tzus make great pets for thousands of families throughout the world.

emperor — a male ruler of an empire

The long, silky hair of shih tzus reminded early Chinese emperors of lion fur.

5

Many dog lovers want to raise a puppy. When choosing a shih tzu, it's a good idea to contact a shih tzu breeder. Responsible breeders work to improve the breed and pride themselves on meeting the American Kennel Club (AKC) **breed standard**. The dogs these breeders raise usually have excellent health and good personalities.

Although most breeders have only the healthiest, highest quality dogs, you should still ask questions. You'll want to find out if the puppy's parents had any health problems. You'll also want to know if the puppy has been examined by a veterinarian.

Some people are not interested in raising a puppy. Shih tzus adjust easily, so grown dogs can still bond with new owners. Many dog lovers contact their local animal shelter or rescue organization to find a shih tzu. Also, breeders are often willing to adopt out adult dogs that are retired from showing and breeding.

breed standard — the physical features of a breed that judges look for in a dog show

At 12 weeks, a shih tzu puppy is old enough to go to a new home.

CHAPTER 2

HISTORY OF SHIH TZUS

In Tibet and China, followers of **Buddhism** honor the lion as a strong religious symbol. Often, Buddha's message is referred to as the lion's roar. Since lions do not live in or near Tibet, the Buddhist monks there bred dogs to look like lions. They bred several breeds including the Lhasa apso and Tibetan terrier.

The Buddhist leader in Tibet is called the Dalai Lama. In the mid-1600s, the Dalai Lama gave some of Tibet's smallest dogs to the Chinese emperor. These little dogs were the ancestors of the modern shih tzu.

Buddhism — a religion based on the teachings of Buddha; Buddhists believe that people may live many lives in different bodies.

Today, Buddhist monks still own Tibetan Lhasa apsos like they did years ago.

9

In China, the dogs were raised in the emperor's home, called the Forbidden City. Palace servants took charge of breeding the dogs. They competed to breed dogs the emperor would like. They wanted to be rewarded with higher status and more authority.

During this time, Pekingese and other dogs were bred with the Tibetan dogs. This breeding produced dogs that were different from the Tibetan lion dogs. They were smaller and had different markings on their fur. This new breed was the modern shih tzu.

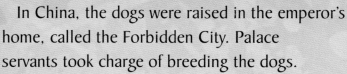

EDGE FACT

In 2007, shih tzus were the ninth most popular breed according to the AKC.

The Pekingese was one of the breeds used to create the shih tzu.

In the mid-1900s, communists viewed pets as a sign of wealth in China.

No Pets Allowed!

After the Chinese Revolution (1927–1949) was fought, the Communist Party led the country. Communists viewed wealthy people as greedy and lazy. Communists saw pets as a symbol of wealth. All pets were forbidden.

Because of this law, shih tzus disappeared from China by the late 1950s. Fortunately, in the 1920s and 1930s, Europeans had brought some shih tzus to England, Ireland, and Scandinavia. Modern shih tzus can be traced back to 13 dogs that left China around this time and a Pekingese **crossbreed** from England.

crossbreed — a breed created by mating two different dog breeds

The Secret Gets Out

It didn't take long for Europeans to fall in love with the shih tzu. Quickly, the breed spread to Germany and even Australia. During World War II (1939–1945), American soldiers stationed in Europe brought shih tzus back to the United States with them. The AKC allowed shih tzus to compete for dog show championships in 1969. Shih tzus quickly began winning show titles. Today, shih tzus and the owners who love them can be found throughout the world.

Playful and friendly shih tzus are popular family pets.

CHAPTER 3

A FUN, FRIENDLY PET

What is a shih tzu's job? Unlike many other breeds, the shih tzu does not help people hunt, herd sheep, or guard people's homes. The shih tzu was bred simply to be a companion.

As a companion dog, a shih tzu is outgoing and friendly toward all people. It snuggles in its owner's lap. It greets strangers with a wag of the tail. Shih tzus are gentle with small children, who can sometimes be rough with dogs. Shih tzus are too friendly to be used as watchdogs. Intruders may end up being attacked only with dog kisses from a family's shih tzu!

A shih tzu's favorite spot is its owner's lap.

A shih tzu holds its head high. Its tail curls over its back.

Shih tzus can seem arrogant. They walk confidently and hold their heads high. Shih tzus can also be stubborn. Some breeds live to please their masters. But shih tzus may prefer for their masters to please them. They may not always follow commands. Owners need to be firm when training a shih tzu.

Physical Traits

Shih tzus are known for having a lot of hair. Their long, flowing double coats may be gold, silver, black, liver, or blue. Liver is a reddish-brown color. Blue is a gray-blue color. The coats can also have varied markings. For example, dogs can be solid, masked, or **parti-color**. A masked shih tzu has darker hair on its face.

parti-color — having a dominant color with patches of one or more other colors

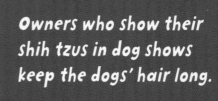

Shih tzu hair does not shed seasonally like other dogs' fur. Instead shih tzus lose small amounts of hair throughout the year just like people do.

Shih tzus are known for their small size. They are usually 8 to 11 inches (20 to 28 centimeters) tall at the shoulders. Shih tzus are slightly longer than they are tall. They usually weigh between 9 and 16 pounds (4 and 7 kilograms).

A shih tzu's round, broad head is held high. Its large, round eyes show friendliness and trust. Its ears appear to blend in with its head. The dog's short, square muzzle may have a slight underbite. But it does not look pushed in or wrinkly.

21

CHAPTER 4

CARING FOR A SHIH TZU

Caring for a shih tzu involves feeding, grooming, and training it. Puppies should be trained as early as possible. To teach a shih tzu good manners, owners should set firm rules. When everyone in the family enforces the rules, the dog understands how to behave. If a shih tzu is allowed to misbehave, bad behavior is reinforced.

A strong-willed shih tzu may resist housebreaking. Puppies rarely soil where they sleep, so crate training is an excellent way to housebreak a shih tzu. When a puppy is left alone, it stays in a comfortable plastic or metal dog crate. Owners then take the puppy outside to relieve itself frequently, especially after eating, playing, or sleeping. In this way, puppies learn to go to the bathroom outdoors.

All dogs should know how to obey the command "sit."

Shih tzus are playful and love to show off. A few fun and easy tricks to teach a shih tzu are roll over, speak, shake hands, and fetch. To teach these skills, it is important to reward a puppy with treats, praise, and affection.

Grooming

Shih tzus require a lot of grooming. Brushing is a daily task. Because dirty coats tangle easily, shih tzus need baths every one to three weeks. After a bath, the coat should be conditioned, brushed, and blown dry. After each bath, the coat should be trimmed.

After a bath, a shih tzu needs its long hair blown dry.

A shih tzu should be
brushed every day.

If a shih tzu is not brushed frequently, its hair may become severely tangled, or matted. A matted shih tzu should never be bathed. Bathing makes the mats almost impossible to remove. If much of the coat is tangled, the dog may need to visit a professional groomer. At worst, the dog's coat may need to be closely shaved.

Feeding

A quality dry dog food keeps a shih tzu healthy. It also keeps its hair shiny. Young puppies should receive four meals per day. Six-month-old puppies usually eat twice a day. Adult shih tzus can be fed one or two meals a day.

EDGE FACT

Many owners put their shih tzu's hair in a topknot. A topknot keeps the hair out of a shih tzu's eyes.

Exercise and Vet Care

Shih tzus require less exercise than many dog breeds. Still, playful shih tzus need and enjoy daily walks and playtime. Exercise helps keep them from becoming overweight.

Veterinarians help owners care for their shih tzus. At a yearly check up, dogs receive vaccinations. A vet can also spay or neuter pets. Owners choose to have these operations on their pets to keep the animals from ever having offspring. Spaying and neutering also helps prevent some types of cancer.

Shih tzus can live into their teens. So bringing a little lion dog into your home is a long-term commitment. Still, this commitment is a rewarding one. For hundreds of years, the playful and loving shih tzu has given companionship and joy to its owners.

Shih tzus enjoy playing outdoors with their owners.

Glossary

breed (BREED) — a certain kind of animal within an animal group; breed also means to mate and raise a certain kind of dog or other animal.

breeder (BREE-duhr) — someone who breeds and raises dogs or other animals

breed standard (BREED STAN-derd) — the physical features of a breed that judges look for in a dog show

Buddhism (BOO-di-zuhm) — a religion based on the teachings of Buddha; Buddhists believe that people may live many lives in different bodies.

Communist Party (KAM-yuh-nist PAHR-tee) — a political party that believes all land, houses, and businesses should belong to the government

crossbreed (KROSS-breed) — a breed created by mating two different dog breeds

emperor (EM-puhr-uhr) — a male ruler of an empire; Chinese emperors made all decisions for the people they ruled.

markings (MAR-kings) — patches of color on fur

mat (MAT) — a thick, tangled mass of hair

monk (MUHNGK) — a man who lives in a religious community and promises to devote his life to his religion

parti-color (PAR-tee-KUHL-ur) — having a dominant color with patches of one or more other colors

vaccination (vak-suh-NAY-shuhn) — a shot of medicine that protects animals from a disease

Read More

Dennis-Bryan, Kim. *Puppy Care: A Guide to Loving and Nurturing Your Pet*. New York: DK, 2004.

Gray, Susan H. *Shih Tzus*. Domestic Dogs. Chanhassen, Minn.: Child's World, 2007.

Internet Sites

FactHound offers a safe, fun way to find Internet sites related to this book. All of the sites on FactHound have been researched by our staff.

Here's how:

1. Visit *www.facthound.com*
2. Choose your grade level.
3. Type in this book ID **1429619503** for age-appropriate sites. You may also browse subjects by clicking on letters, or by clicking on pictures and words.
4. Click on the **Fetch It** button.

FactHound will fetch the best sites for you!

Index